# The Road to Salvation
# The Welfare TRAP

I0416062

Anthony W. Antolic

# DEDICATION

This book is dedicated to all of those people who lost every the in Hurricane Katrina, but more importantly to all those who did not give up in her wake.

# CONTENTS

# ACKNOWLEDGMENTS

Heartfelt thanks to the countless people who I have spoken to while doing this research. Further credit is given in my research notes and my citations.

# 1 CHAPTER
## HOW CAN WELFARE BE A TRAP?

For many the Welfare system may seem harmless enough, but if you have ever spent any time as a recipient of its programs, you would most likely agree that there are two human reactions that results from being on Welfare. Those reactions are a feeling of relief and anger. There is nothing in between?

The recipient feels like a weight is taken off of him or her, because there is finally food in the house. However, there is a stigma attached to Welfare that most of us who are on it or have been on it should maintain. No one should ever want to be on government assistance. We should be ashamed that we are not doing enough to support our families: for if we become complacent and willing to comply with the rules that power hungry bureaucracy who needs participants to survive, otherwise the largest employer in America will not be able to justify the tax dollars, we become part of the problem.

The rules, as stupid as the sound, are set up so people feel trapped in the system. Restrictions on how much money a participant can save and still qualify for the program as well as how much you can work if at all, may have been designed to offset abuses of the program: but these same rules end up trapping many Americans in the system. Think about it, if there is no weaning off period, a man who was once unable to work due to an injury starts to get better, but his benefits are his only source of income he would not do anything to hurt his lively hood, especially if that man is told that once he starts to go back to work he will not only loose the financial benefits but the medical that is much more important to recover from his injury. Therein lies the Trap.

It is the hoops that someone has to jump through that truly creates the trap. An argument can be made that the Welfare System forces you to make a choice between what the needs of a family are and the demands of the government are. I have spoken to many people over the years who have been forced to turn down jobs to continue to qualify for welfare, so their family member could get the medical attention they need. In such a case, the system is not allowing the participant's household to bring in more than $2000.00 a month before taxes and the new job would have made two much money. After seeing such circumstantial evidence one is forced to ask, "does the government truly want people to get out of the system?

## FreeTrade to Support Welfare

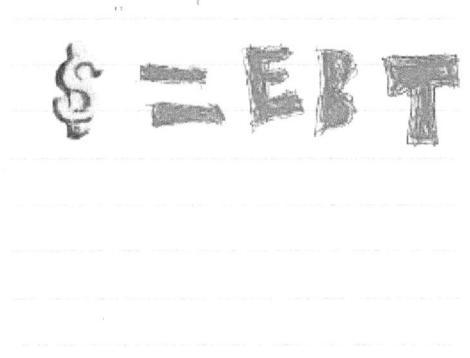

The unfortunate reality for the American government is that over 1/3 of the American workforce is in some way affiliated with government social programs. Think about it, the public schools, department of corrections and even hospitals are all in some way under the umbrella of what is commonly known as the Welfare system. In other words, the American government has too much to lose if they start to help people off of Government Assistance.

As sad as it may be, the unwritten practices of such Secret Combinations as Child Protective Services, the Department Social Health Services, as well as the Food and Drug Administration work together to force otherwise healthy children into chemical dependency, to perpetuation the justified existence of their organizations for the benefit of the tax payer. Remember, at this point in history America would have to completely. Restructure our economy if we really wanted to help the people that these programs effect, therefore, it just seems cheaper in the short term to breed drug addictions in our youth and act like we are fighting against drug use.

When a member of my family was 16 years old, her father did not know how to handle her behavior so he took he to their local quack. The so call doctor used extraordinary means to proscribe over 100 mg. over what could be lawfully proscribed. Still after her shrink could get 2 more signatures he was able to use the child as a lab rat. Now more than 20 year later, she has symptoms of withdrawal rather than any kind of psychotic episode. The quacks mission was successful, now she is totally dependent on the government for medications that she never would have needed.

If she would have been diagnosed today with the same symptomology, she would have been said to have ADD compounded by adolescent growing pains and things would be vary diffident for her. But instead of trying to fix a problem, many doctors just write a new script, thereby making America one of, if not the most heavily medicated countries in the world; and why not addiction breads complacency.

We should have known that America's economy was in trouble, when signs like this started to become common place. I began to notice that my home town of Vancouver Washington was flying more EBT signs than Help Wanted. So I asked myself, "is there a correlation between Food-Stamps and a dying economy?" I is Food-Stamps the cause or the effect of our lack of Jobs?

A Liberal piece of scum would tell you that, it is not fare that there are not enough jobs to go around. Well let's explore that argument. The symbol for justice has long been the scales. In fact it is no accident that the 3rd. Horseman of the book of Revelation is reported to be holding the scales of Judgment.

You see Famine is the angle of divine judgment, it is not his voice that is heard crying out, "A ration of wheat costs a day's pay and three rations of barley cost a day's pay. But don't touch the olive oil or the wine" (Revolution 6: 5-6 Page 393), the voice was fume sinners of the world, pleading for our addictions to be left alone. Seeing more EBT signs than Help Wanted, says that Americans have become addicted to our not having to work for anything.

Even if those of us who want work succeed in getting out of the trap many of us would have to break the laws of the land to do it. Once again Justice is about balance and not about being fare. Unless you are one of the few that can find a job that puts you in a higher tax bracket, than you were in while on the social service programs, that can offer your family medical and other benefits such as a retirement plan that will keep you off of SSI-R or Social Security Income for your Retirement, you will always be part of the Welfare Trap. The only way out for many of us is to hide money from the government.

## 2 CHAPTER
## BREAKING THE LAW TO PROTECT YOUR FAMILIES FUTURE

"Governments are instituted among Men, deriving their just powers from the co cent of the governed. That whenever any Form of Government becomes destructive to these ends, it is the [necessary] RIGHT of the People to alter or abolish [said government]" (the Declaration of Independence). (Rossiter DI, 528)

I know, Mormon doctrine says that we should blindly follow the laws of the land. Well Thomas Jefferson said, "It is a citizen's duty to overthrow a broken government and put a new guard in its place." Mormons feel that means to remove the elect from their office by electing someone else. However, I know that as a Sniper I helped manipulate the outcomes of many elections and even made governments turn to dust. Thomas Jefferson used the word "abolish" not for reference to a coming election but rather to start over with a new guard, for an election only brings in the next generation of corruption. Therefore, I don't believe in democracy. I have found that some of the most useless people we have in the fight against the inevitable destructive powers of the elected are those who sit and pray but do nothing to help their prayers along.

Contrary to popular belief, people do not exist to serve the government, which seems to be a common misperception that many people have. I was raised to always ask, "Who is making the laws of the land?" Here is an example, if there was a large population of Mormons in Germany in 1930, would the LDS members in the country at the time, would they have been a part of the solution or the problem. Remember the will of Adolf Hitler was the law of the land: therefore the question must be asked, "would the Mormons have worked to over through the Chancellor of Germany?"

Hasn't any one thought about why Karl Marx once said that "Christianity is an opiate for the masses." Could it be that he saw how the blind respect for authority made it easier for him to control the group than any other faith tradition? All that I know for sure is that America was never meant to be a democracy, for those masses are easily manipulated. If America was meant to be a democracy and not the Republic for which our flag stands, our Constitution would about read in Article 4 - Section 4, "the United States shall guarantee to every State in the Union a Republican form of Government" (Rossiter Con, 554).

The reason I bring the Republic up or any of the content of this chapter up is simple, a republic is defined by its charter, in America the Constitution is the Republic's charter. The Constitution was written to protect the rights of each individual. In the first chapter I talked about how much of the population is being oppressed due to their involvement in American social programs. I also talked about how this oppression is intentional.

As this chapter unfolds I well talk about how people break the law to protect the future of their families. Remember the question about Hitler and the Mormons; ask yourself the same question as you read about these families. The standard answer is that Mormons would fallow God's law before the law of the land; therefore, anything that is not in line with Natural Law should be irrelevant.

The law or regulations that trap people into the Welfare system are after thoughts of the organizational bylaws. Most of them were put in place to protect the taxpayer's money from fraud and violating them has harsh penalties. However, every law has its loop wholes.

The first couple I am going to introduce you to, was married for 15 years. Mike is a retired welder who lost his leg and half of his other foot in an industrial accident. His wife Kate was told last year that the two of them would be better off financially if they divorced and just lived together. They did get that divorce and their benefits from the state doubled the day the divorce was final.

Mike and Kate have been forced to live off of the tax payers for the past 5 years. Like many families who have family members who need government assistance, Mike and Kate Henderson are choosing to live in sin according most religions to be allowed to make a living wage and still keep the benefits that Mike needs to receive the medical attention he needs.

Once Franklin D. Roosevelt instituted what he called the New Deal, American morality and basic family values began to be attacked. Social programs should not be rewarding signal women to breed out of wedlock just to justify next year's grant, but this is what happens in America daily. I met a homeless teen named Mandy. She decided to become a prostitute in the hopes that she would get pregnant, because she knew that the chances of her getting into a government subsidized home is much higher if she had a child.

If you remember the scales that the third horseman of the Apocalypse holds in Revelation, 6:5-6 is a symbol of our proprieties getting thrown askew. Instead of perpetuating the problem by teaching the next generation how to pilfer the tax payers, maybe we should punish the Welfare Whore by removing the child and putting him or her up for adoption, and making the harlot the subject of a public stoning. Many would say that killing her is too harsh but at the same time our society is rewarding prostitution and condemning innovation.
I say this because we reward those who don't want to work and condemn those of us that do.

Most states in the union have adopted the need based welfare model. This model decides your benefits according to your gross wages and nothing more. The model is said to deduct from your benefit according to how much you paid in to your taxes. But if this was true you would not be punished for working, rather than getting more money in your Welfare check you have more deducted from your check. Thus encouraging people to work less and get paid more. If a person truly wants to get off welfare they go back to school and learn a skill.

John is currently attending college to become a mechanic through a program the state unemployment department offers. But there is another problem with in the Welfare system. The public school systems are one of the most over looked parts of public assistance. Yet, they are by far the most important player in the Welfare Agenda. Most states get upset with parents when they choose to take on the responsibility of educating and raising their own children. The reason for this is clear.

The public schools play the role of intentionally misguiding and under-educating our youth. If this was not the case, the excessive vacations and premature graduation into the workforce would not be a reality. The perceived rule of the public education system and its reality are two very different things. Most people think that public education is to indoctrinate our youth into the workforce. The truth is that the education system's purpose is to access and profile each student so the government knows who will contribute and who will become a social liability. If this was not the case, parents would not get so much grief from the law for trying to teach their kids right.

My friends Darrel and Mary were charged with child neglect, because their school district told CPS that they never registered their kids for school the year Mary decided to home school her two kids. Mary who is a devoted mother as well as a practicing Attorney, who graduated from Cambridge University, knew that she could do a far better job educating her children than some underpaid bureaucratic fool who has no vested interest in their futures.

After taking the city of Vancouver to court both Mary and Darrel began going from church to church talking about why they had to win the fight for their children future. "America's children are living in a cesspool of amorality." Darrel told a group of believers at the annual family conference of 2003 at Saint Joesph's Catholic church in Vancouver Washington.

Darrel was a shop teacher at Mountain View High School, I had him for welding the whole time I went to school there. In 2002 I paid him a visit at school and he expressed his malcontent about the work ethic of his students. "Tony, I enjoyed teaching when you were stilling in school, but theses kids …" I laughed not understanding what he was getting at and said to him, "I am sure you had to put up with the same kind of stuff when we where in school." Mr. Middles replied, "you guys wanted to learn and you where willing to work but these kids are a different animal."

I was eager to know what my friend meant by his last statement although I was sure that I already knew. Darrel when on to tell me that this generation wants everything handed to them and how the schools are not helping the situation. Only 9 months later, Darrel Middles retired from the Evergreen School District. It was not until I would hear him speak at Saint Joseph's that I would learn the whole story behind his abjection against the public school system.

Darrel and his wife Mary, saw a pattern that was emerging in the school systems even 15 years before I met them. If you think about it you have seen them too. Why is public education always the first to be cut in the budget? Could it be that the real reason we have public schools is to wean the next generation into the welfare trap? This would be the only reason that I could see that children get advanced to the next grade with out being able to read.

I graduated at the bottom of my class in 1993. It was not until my second years of college that some people took the time to teach me what should have been done by kinder-garden. I mean let's face it adult illiteracy is an epidemic in America, which does nothing to help with the unemployment rate. However, it does help the largest sector of the American economy maintain its self. No child left behind is a crock. The Welfare system is will to break the law to pull as many people into it as possible, so parents must be willing to break the law to protect their children from CPS and other branches of this Leviathan who has a. Strangle hold on America.

# 3 CHAPTER
## THE GHOSTS OF THE PAST

We all have ghosts in our past, you know the bad choices we made that we don't real want to admit too. For me the ghost is nothing that I have done at least intentionally. Its like the saying goes, "you don't pick your parents. I was born John Kelly Nash, in true Romonie tradition my Grandfather wanted me to take my mother's maiden name. But even before my first memories, my mother changed my name against my Grandfather's wishes. When I learned of it I did not understand why my mother wanted the separation from her family. But after 09/11/2001, I started having problems not just getting a job but all so keeping one as well. With the in statement of the Patriot Act, companies began to do much more in dept background checks.

It got so bad that I would be employed and working doing a good job and I get called into the office, at which point I would get fired. Most employers in Oregon and Washington don't have to tell you why you have been let go, so I would go from job to job in this endless cycle. It was not until a coworker showed me how to run my own background that I realized that I was screwed. Homeland Security Flagged me as a "Potential Domestic Threat." Most employers don't even know what that means, so they run  my background again.  Once again the flag shows up and I get fired. Now I. Know what it feels like to be a convicted felon in America and no crime has been committed,  on my part any way.

 For many Americans ignoring the past is not so simple as just not talking about it. Whether you admit it you or not, the Department of Corrections or DOC, is also a vary lucrative asset to the Welfare Trap. A felon will not have a fighting chance on the outside unless they get lucky along the way. While much of what I am talking about is human nature, more of it than not is through design.

Many of the people that I have worked with other the years, can't even get an apartment thanks to how their background check looks. We can contribute much of the felon's problem to the Calvinistic roots of American culture. Theses same roots is where we can find the roots of the regulations that keep people trapped in the Welfare system. Theologians call it the doctrine of Predestination.

"The Free Will problem or Predestination, is an argument about what the nature of free agency is in relation to the origins and conditions of responsible behavior" (Audi, 326). John Calvin and his Puritan followers believed that humans are only as free to make a choice as his or her external environment will allow. The argument does nothing to allow for personal growth, because the person is believed to be so heavily influenced by external factors that no choice is made by the person but rather by God himself. In the most basic terms, Predestination holds that every event that has and will happen was predetermined by God. In philosophical terms the event solution or the idea that one thing effects the outcome of another, such as the loss of a job pushing some one toward committing a crime, is thought to keep people in poverty thus justifying the hoops that the Welfare system has designed to keep people trapped in the system. Like it or not, politics and religion are one in the same in a Theocracy and remember America was founded by Calvinists.

Beyond not being able to find an apartment or a job, a person's credit score is also a factor in every day life in America. While the banks have nothing to do with the Welfare system its self, the concept of a credit score has much to do with the Welfare system. The ghosts from our past come back to haunt us every time we go to rent an apartment or by a car. Think about it, what is your credit score really telling people? Are they asking, does he pay his bills or are they asking does he get in trouble? I think you can answer that for yourself.

The sad fact is that people get trapped in the system due to the choices they made in the past. Our society likes to think that we h Vercher grown past slavery, but the truth is that we must by our freedom by paying back our debts to both God and society. The way we treat felons is wrong. The law says they paid back their debt and set them free. Only to go back to prison because they know there they have shelter and food, which is more than they might have with no one willing to give them a chance to work or a place to stay. Our society creates more crime by not being willing to forgive the ghosts of some ones past. Some one who may have never been back to jail would commit armed robbery, if he is hungry enough and cold enough to want to go back to jail. Jesus wants us to "love our neighbor" (Mark, 12:31), maybe it is time to do so.

I have never committed a crime, I have never killed any one with out orders. I served for the United Nations Peace Keeping forces and yet due to the fact that my family has blown up banks and bridges and other random things in Ireland. America treats me like a criminal. Many times the thought has crossed my mind to just become the criminal that America say I am. After all out side of prison I am going through same same things that a felon would, so I can see how a convict would feel that he or see would better off in prison. In truth, unless society begins to treat the ex-con better, we may as well just kill them rather than releasing them. The truth is most of the homeless we see are in the same position I described.

In most co unities it is illegal to bee homeless. Therefore the ex-con who can get a job or an apartment is put right back in there system.Thus the Welfare System traps the same right back in to it.

# 4 CHAPTER
# BLESSINGS THROUGH HARDSHIP

I have found that through all the hard times that my wife and I are forced to live with, we see some amazing blessings come our way. Even before I met Kansa, I was using the fact that I work as a professional Temp, to help God's people. I have told my readers about the time I spent in the South helping with clean up and other thing after Katrina, well I would not have the freedom to do that if I was working a real job. Kansa and I have a stronger relationship because we choose to face the challenges of our lives together.

Our blessings come with many sacrifices. As I get older, I can't do some of the things that I once did. I will not be jumping out of any helicopters any time soon, but while I was able to do that lives were saved.

Now Kansa and I work together to make ends meat. We work as Temps so if any one needs help we can free up our day so we can help. Although Kansa's health is not the best, she always seems to be willing to offer a hand. It is my belief that God needs us where we are.

However, for a long time I was bitter about the restrictions that the government puts on us. If I work too much Kansa's Medical insurance is forfeit, but if I don't work enough, we are homeless. Therefore, I play this stupid game of priorities and pray that I am right. Most of the time I am just grateful to have a job that pays our bills.

For years I have worked as a Temporary Employee, with no hope of ever being hired, due to how my background check always comes back. I have committed no crimes, but due to family affiliations, no one wants to give me a chance. The few jobs that have been offered to me, can not sustain life much less pay my bills. As a result of my employment situation that began with Interim who grandfathered me in to Kelley's Services, a and then Express Employment Professionals, who currently has the contract, I have earned the trust of the AWC Employees who work the closest with me. I have the recommendations of Aaron Smith, the yard lead at Terminal 5 in Portland Oregon, as well as the fallowing AWC Employees, Pete Castro, Matt Olson, Garry May, Anna Christ, and their boss Duane Werbowski, who also work at the same Faculty. I have worked myself into a leadership position over as many as 40 temps at a time and done many long term special projects such as landscaping and remodeling the facility. However, as time has passed, even though both terminal 5 and 6 fight over who gets to use me, it has become clear that AWC will never higher me. I feel trapped in the position I am in. AWC works me too much to find a full time position with anything other than a staffing service. As a result of my frustration with Auto Warehousing's lack of desire to give my a job even after 15 years of dedicated service, during which time I have never missed a day of work that I was scheduled or even been late, I will be looking for other employment depending on the outcome of this application, although I know No one will hire me. Yet, I am lucky to have a job.

Anthony W. Antolic

# ABOUT THE AUTHOR

Anthony Antolic was born  Johnathan Kelly Nash. His mother changed his name before Anthony was old enough to remember. His grandfather's influence on him has Anthony questioning everything. After Anthony married his wife Kansa, he was forced to learn about the endless Black Whole known as American Social Programs. His personal hardships are also examined as he talks about his time helping out with Hurricane Katrina.

By comparing notes with others in a similar situation, Mr. Antolic soon realized what so many before him had found, that the system is designed to keep you trapped. Along the way Anthony discovered that his name change plays a large part in the struggles that he and his wife live through from day to day.

"You can call it conspiracy, or even paranoia, but no one can argue the fact that American Social Services are there largest employer in America next to only the Department of Defense. Just imagine what would happen if that taxes to fund these programs could no longer be justified!"

# BIBLIOGRAPHY

Note:            books are listed in the order which they are first cited.

Rossiter Clinton, "The Federalist Papers," New American Library, a division of Penguin Books, © 2003, ISBN# 978-0-451-5281-0

Note:         (Rossiter H)     =      Alexander Hamilton

         (Rossiter M)     =      James Madison

         (Rossiter J)      =      John Jay

         (Rossiter DI)    =      The Declaration of Independence

         (Rossiter Con)  =      The Constitution

Audi Robert, the Cambridge of Philosophy, Second Edition, Cambridge University Press, ©1999, ISBN# 978-0-521-63722-0

The New American Bible {Saint Joseph Edition}, Catholic Book Publishing Company, © 1991

www.ingramcontent.com/pod-product-compliance
Lightning Source LLC
Chambersburg PA
CBHW071022290526
45795CB00005B/1889